Learn Latin with Beginner Stories - Colloquia Dialogues

HypLern Interlinear Project
www.hyplern.com

First edition: 2025, September

Author: Mathurin Cordier
Translation: Dr Th. van den End
Foreword: Camilo Andrés Bonilla Carvajal PhD

Translation and interlinear formatting © 2025 Bermuda Word. All rights
reserved.

ISBN: 978-1-988830-71-1

kees@hyplern.com
www.hyplern.com

Learn Latin with Beginner Stories - Colloquia Dialogues

Interlinear Latin to English

Author
Mathurin Cordier

Translation
Dr Th. van den End

HypLern Interlinear Project
www.hyplern.com

The HypLern Method

Learning a foreign language should not mean leafing through page after page in a bilingual dictionary until one's fingertips begin to hurt. Quite the contrary, through everyday language use, friendly reading, and direct exposure to the language we can get well on our way towards mastery of the vocabulary and grammar needed to read native texts. In this manner, learners can be successful in the foreign language without too much study of grammar paradigms or rules. Indeed, Seneca expresses in his sixth epistle that "Longum iter est per praecepta, breve et efficax per exempla[1]."

The HypLern series constitutes an effort to provide a highly effective tool for experiential foreign language learning. Those who are genuinely interested in utilizing original literary works to learn a foreign language do not have to use conventional graded texts or adapted versions for novice readers. The former only distort the actual essence of literary works, while the latter are highly reduced in vocabulary and relevant content. This collection aims to bring the lively experience of reading stories as directly told by their very authors to foreign language learners.

Most excited adult language learners will at some point seek their teachers' guidance on the process of learning to read in the foreign language rather than seeking out external opinions. However, both teachers and learners lack a general reading technique or strategy. Oftentimes, students undertake the reading task equipped with nothing more than a bilingual dictionary, a grammar book, and lots of courage. These efforts often end in frustration as the student builds mis-constructed nonsensical sentences after many hours spent on an aimless translation drill.

Consequently, we have decided to develop this series of interlinear translations intended to afford a comprehensive edition of unabridged texts. These texts are presented as they were originally written with no changes in word choice or order. As a result, we have a translated piece conveying the true meaning under every word from the original work. Our readers receive then two books in just one volume: the original version and its translation.

The reading task is no longer a laborious exercise of patiently decoding unclear and seemingly complex paragraphs. What's more, reading becomes an enjoyable and meaningful process of cultural, philosophical and linguistic learning. Independent learners can then acquire expressions and vocabulary while understanding pragmatic and socio-cultural dimensions of the target language by reading in it rather than reading about it.

Our proposal, however, does not claim to be a novelty. Interlinear translation is as old as the Spanish tongue, e.g. "glosses of [Saint] Emilianus", interlinear bibles in Old German, and of course James Hamilton's work in the 1800s. About the latter, we remind the readers, that as a revolutionary freethinker he promoted the publication of Greco-Roman classic works and further pieces in diverse languages. His effort, such as ours, sought to lighten the exhausting task of looking words up in large glossaries as an educational practice: "if there is any thing which fills reflecting men with melancholy and regret, it is the waste of mortal time, parental money, and puerile happiness, in the present method of pursuing Latin and Greek[2]".

Additionally, another influential figure in the same line of thought as Hamilton was John Locke. Locke was also the philosopher and translator of the Fabulae AEsopi in an interlinear plan. In 1600, he was already suggesting that interlinear texts, everyday communication, and use of the target language could be the most appropriate ways to achieve language learning:

> ...the true and genuine Way, and that which I would propose, not only as the easiest and best, wherein a Child might, without pains or Chiding, get a Language which others are wont to be whipt for at School six or seven Years together...[3]

---

1   "The journey is long through precepts, but brief and effective through examples". Seneca, Lucius Annaeus. (1961) Ad Lucilium Epistulae Morales, vol. I. London: W. Heinemann.

2   In: Hamilton, James (1829?) History, principles, practice and results of the Hamiltonian system, with answers to the Edinburgh and Westminster reviews; A lecture delivered at Liverpool; and instructions for the use of the books published on the system. Londres: W. Aylott and Co., 8, Pater Noster Row. p. 29.

3   In: Locke, John. (1693) Some thoughts concerning education. Londres: A. and J. Churchill. pp. 196-7.

Who can benefit from this edition?

We identify three kinds of readers, namely, those who take this work as a search tool, those who want to learn a language by reading authentic materials, and those attempting to read writers in their original language. The HypLern collection constitutes a very effective instrument for all of them.

1. For the first target audience, this edition represents a search tool to connect their mother tongue with that of the writer's. Therefore, they have the opportunity to read over an original literary work in an enriching and certain manner.
2. For the second group, reading every word or idiomatic expression in its actual context of use will yield a strong association between the form, the collocation, and the context. This will have a direct impact on long term learning of passive vocabulary, gradually building genuine reading ability in the original language. This book is an ideal companion not only to independent learners but also to those who take lessons with a teacher. At the same time, the continuous feeling of achievement produced during the process of reading original authors both stimulates and empowers the learner to study[1].
3. Finally, the third kind of reader will notice the same benefits as the previous ones. The proximity of a word and its translation in our interlinear texts is a step further from other collections, such as the Loeb Classical Library. Although their works might be considered the most famous in this genre, the presentation of texts on opposite pages hinders the immediate link between words and their semantic equivalence in our native tongue (or one we have a strong mastery of).

---

1 Some further ways of using the present work include:

1. As you progress through the stories, focus less on the lower line (the English translation). Instead, try to read through the upper line, staying in the foreign language as long as possible.
2. Even if you find glosses or explanatory footnotes about the mechanics of the language, you should make your own hypotheses on word formation and syntactical functions in a sentence. Feel confident about inferring your own language rules and test them progressively. You can also take notes concerning those idiomatic expressions or special language usage that calls your attention for later study.
3. As soon as you finish each text, check the reading in the original version (with no interlinear or parallel translation). This will fulfil the main goal of this

collection: bridging the gap between readers and original literary works, training them to read directly and independently.

Why interlinear?

Conventionally speaking, tiresome reading in tricky and exhausting circumstances has been the common definition of learning by texts. This collection offers a friendly reading format where the language is not a stumbling block anymore. Contrastively, our collection presents a language as a vehicle through which readers can attain and understand their authors' written ideas.

While learning to read, most people are urged to use the dictionary and distinguish words from multiple entries. We help readers skip this step by providing the proper translation based on the surrounding context. In so doing, readers have the chance to invest energy and time in understanding the text and learning vocabulary; they read quickly and easily like a skilled horseman cantering through a book.

Thereby we stress the fact that our proposal is not new at all. Others have tried the same before, coming up with evident and substantial outcomes. Certainly, we are not pioneers in designing interlinear texts. Nonetheless, we are nowadays the only, and doubtless, the best, in providing you with interlinear foreign language texts.

Handling instructions

Using this book is very easy. Each text should be read at least three times in order to explore the whole potential of the method. The first phase is devoted to comparing words in the foreign language to those in the mother tongue. This is to say, the upper line is contrasted to the lower line as the following example shows:

III.	PRO	TANTILLO	AGENDAM	GRATIAM?
3	For	so little a thing	must be given	thanks

The second phase of reading focuses on capturing the meaning and sense of the original text. As readers gain practice with the method, they should be able to focus on the target language without getting distracted by the translation. New users of the method, however, may find it helpful to cover the translated lines with a piece of paper as illustrated in the image below. Subsequently, they try to understand the meaning of every word, phrase, and entire sentences in the target language itself, drawing on the translation only when necessary. In this phase, the reader should resist the temptation to look at the translation for every word. In doing so, they will find that they are able to understand a good portion of the text by reading directly in the target language, without the crutch of the translation. This is the skill we are looking to train: the ability to read and understand native materials and enjoy them as native speakers do, that being, directly in the original language.

III. PRO TANTILLO AGENDAM GRATIAM?

3   For   so little

In the final phase, readers will be able to understand the meaning of the text when reading it without additional help. There may be some less common words and phrases which have not cemented themselves yet in the reader's brain, but the majority of the story should not pose any problems. If desired, the reader can use an SRS or some other memorization method to learning these straggling words.

III. PRO TANTILLO AGENDAM GRATIAM?

Above all, readers will not have to look every word up in a dictionary to read a text in the foreign language. This otherwise wasted time will be spent concentrating on their principal interest. These new readers will tackle authentic texts while learning their vocabulary and expressions to use in further communicative (written or oral) situations. This book is just one work from an overall series with the same purpose. It really helps those who are afraid of having "poor vocabulary" to feel confident about reading directly in the language. To all of them and to all of you, welcome to the amazing experience of living a foreign language!

Additional tools

Check out shop.hyplern.com or contact us at info@hyplern.com for free mp3s (if available) and free empty (untranslated) versions of the eBooks that we have on offer.

For some of the older eBooks and paperbacks we have Windows, iOS and Android apps available that, next to the interlinear format, allow for a pop-up format, where hovering over a word or clicking on it gives you its meaning. The apps also have any mp3s, if available, and integrated vocabulary practice.

Visit the site hyplern.com for the same functionality online. This is where we will be working non-stop to make all our material available in multiple formats, including audio where available, and vocabulary practice.

Table of Contents

Part I

I. DE HONORE PRAECEPTORI PRAESTANDO
1 About   the honour   to the teacher   to be rendered

— Heus tu, praeceptor adest.
    Hey   you   the teacher   is there

— Quid tum?
  What   then

— Respice ad illum.
    Look   at   him

— Quamobrem?
     Why?

— Ut   ei   caput   aperias,   et   venientem
   So that   for him   your head   you may uncover   and   (him) coming

salutes.
may greet

— Ita   decet   facere,   sed   aliud
    So   it becomes   to do   but   (of) something else

cogitabam.
I was thinking

— Tace!
   Hush

II. SCRIBERE FORIS
2   To write   outside

— Cur non scribis?
   Why   not   you write

— Iam   scripsi   meam paginam, tu vero?
   Alfready I have written   my   page   you   but

— Eo scriptum in area.
   I go   to write   in   the yard

— Quid ita?
   Why   so

— Quia serenum est coelum.
   Because   bright   is   the sky

— Festina, tempus   abit,   et mox   exigetur
   Hurry   the time goes by and soon it will be asked

ratio.
(to render) account

III. PRO TANTILLO AGENDAM GRATIAM?
3   For   so little a thing must be given   thanks

— Cur non   reddis   mihi librum?
  Why   not you give back to me   the book

— Exspecta   in   crastinum diem, nondum   satis
   Wait   until of tomorrow the day not yet   enough

 usus   sum.
used (it) I am
        (have)

—   Libenter   exspectabo.
  With pleasure   I will wait

— Referam   tibi gratiam, Deo volente.
  I will bring to you   thanks   God   willing

— Pro tantillo beneficio nullam exspecto gratiam.
  For   so little a good deed not at all I expect   thanks

—   Tamen   est meum agnoscere.
  Nevertheless it is my thing to acknowledge
                (mine)

Part II

IV. VOCATUS A FRATRE
4   Called   by   a brother

— Heus, Caie.
     Hey   Caius

— Quid vis?
     What   do you want

— Arcesseris.
     You are being summoned

— Quis me vocat?
     Who   me   calls

— Frater tuus.
     Brother   your

— Ubi est?
     Where   is he

— Prae   foribus   te   exspectat.
In front of the doors for you   he waits

— Certo   scis   esse fratrem meum?
For certain you know to be brother   my
                    that he is my brother

— Quidni   sciam?   Vidi   illum,   et   sum
Why not I would know I have seen   him   and   have

allocutus.
addressed (him)

— Visam sane quid sit.
I will see sure what it is
                    {coni}

V. DE   IENTACULO
5 About   breakfast

— Vis   ientare   mecum?
Do you want to take breakfast   with me

— Non habeo ientaculum.
Not   I have   a breakfast

— Quid? Non attulisti?
What   Not   have you brought (it)

— Ego   domi   ientaveram.
I   at home   have taken breakfast

— Itane   semper   facis?
So   always   you do

— Minime: sed   quia   bene   mane   surrexeram, sic
The least   but   because   well   early   I had woken up   so
(not at all)

matri   placuit   me tractare.
to (my) mother   it has pleased   me   to take care of

— Prosit   tibi: ego igitur solus ientabo.
Cheers   to you   I   so   alone   will take breakfast

— Et ego   interim   studebo.
And I   I   in the meantime   will study

VI. DE   TUNICULA   INDUENDA
6   About the short tunica   to be put on

— Unde   affers   istam tuniculam?
From where   do you bring   that   short tunica

— A   domo.
From   home

— Quid   vis   facere?
   What   do you want   to do

— Volo induere.
   I want to put it on

— Nunc non   est   mutandi tempus.
   Now   not   (there) is   to change   time

— Quando igitur?
   When   then

—   Cras   mane, cum surges   e   lecto.
   Tomorrow   early   when you rise out of (your) bed

— Bene   mones,   exspectabo.
   Well   you advise (me)   I will wait

VII. DE   PENNIS ACUENDIS
  7   About the feathers to be sharpened
              (pens)

—   Acuistine   pennam?
   Have you sharpened   (your) pen

— Iamdudum.
   long ago already

9

— Qua   forma scripturae?
For what   form   of writing

— Mediocri.
medium

— Maluissem   ad minutas literas.
I would like (it) more for   small   letters

— Debuisti   praedicere.
You should have   said (that) before

— Oblitus   eram.   Parum   refert,   mucronem
Forgotten   I was   Little   it matters   the tip (of the pen)
(had)

facile   mutabo.   I   petitum.
easily   I will change   Go   to fetch it
{supinum peto}

— Sed   ubi   reliquisti?
But   where   did you leave (it)

— Super mensam hypocausti.
On   the table   of the heated room

— In qua parte?
In   which   part

— Ubi studere soleo.
Where to study I am used

Part III

VIII. DE PRAESCRIPTO REPETENDO
8   Of   the provision of   repeating

— Quid agis?
What   are you doing

— Repeto mecum.
I repeat   by myself

— Quid repetis?
What   do you repeat

— Praescriptum hodiernum praeceptoris.
The task   today's   of the teacher

— Tenesne memoria?
Do you keep (it)   by heart

— Sic opinor.
So   I guess

— Repetamus una; sic uterque nostrum rectius
Let us repeat   together   so   both   of us   more rightly

pronuntiabit coram praeceptore.
will pronounce   before   the teacher

— Tu igitur, incipe, qui me provocasti.
You therefore   begin   who   me   you have challenged

— Age, attentus esto, ne me sinas
Come on   attentive   be   that not   me   you allow

aberrare.
go wrong

— Sum promptior ad audiendum quam tu ad
I am   more ready   to   hear   than   you   to

pronuntiandum.
pronounce

IX. MAGISTRO ABSENTE QUIS DOCEBIT?
9   The master   being absent   who   will teach

— Magister, nemo est qui doceat in sexta
Master   nobody   (there) is   who   may teach   in   the sixth
(lowest)

13

classe.
class

— Quid hoc rei est? Ubi est magister
What to that matter there is Where is master
is the matter

Philippus?
Philippus

— Morbo detinetur in lecto.
By illness he is kept in (his) bed

— Qui scis?
How do you know
{quo}

— Nuntiavit quidam ex discipulis eius
Has reported (it) somebody out of pupils his

domesticis.
living in his house

— Dic hypodidascalo meo.
Tell under-teacher my

— Non est in museolo suo.
Not he is in study his

— Qui scis?
How you know
{quo}

— Nam ego ter aut quater pulsavi
For I three times or four times have knocked

ostium.
(on) the door

— Dic primae classis doctori, ut mittat e
Say of the first class to the teacher that he send out of
(highest) (coni) (of)

suis aliquem.
his (pupils) somebody

— Quid si nolit mittere?
What if he is not willing to send (somebody)

— Abi, inepte; an putas eum esse tam
Be off you silly whether you think him to be so

impudentem ut recuset? Abi, propera.
insolent that he would refuse Be off hurry

X. SONUIT HOROLOGIUM
10 Has struck the clock

— Audivistine   horologium?
Haven't you heard   the clock

— Dudum sonuit.
long ago   it has struck

— Dinumerasti   horas?
Have you counted   the hours

— Dinumeravi.
I have counted

— Quota   est?
How many   it is

— Fere sesquiprima.
About   one hour and a half (past noon)

— Instat   igitur   praelectionis   tempus: fac   ut
Is near   so   of the lecture   the time   make   that

paratus sis.
ready   you be

— Ubi   merendam   peredero,   ecce   me
Where   afternoon snack   I will have finished eating   see   me
(when)   (I will be)

paratum.
ready

— Cur meridie non adfuisti nobiscum?
Why at noon not have you been present with us

— Prodieram cum bona venia praeceptoris.
I had gone forth with the good leave of the teacher

— Sed interim sum tibi impedimento.
But in the meantime I am to you to inconvenience
(put) (you)

— Nihil impedis; ne bolum quidem
Not at all you are inconvenient not a dice throw even
(mouthful)

perdidi interpellatione tua.
I have lost by interruption your

— Bene habet; perge, sed matura.
well it has go on but make haste
(is)

XI. AUDIAT, SI VELIT
11 Let (him) hear if he likes

— Iamne tenes quae reddenda sunt
Already you hold the things which to be rendered are
(know)

hora   tertia?
in the hour   third

— Teneo.
    I hold

— Ego quoque.
    I   too
  (me)

— Ergo confabulemur paulisper.
    So   let us talk together a little while

— Sed si   intervenerit   observator,   putabit
    But if will have come between   the observer   he will think
                                     (supervisor)

nos garrire.
us   to talk

— Quid   times,   ubi   nihil   timendum est? Si
    Why   do you fear where nothing to be feared   is   If
                     (when)

    venerit,   non deprehendet nos in   otio,
he will have come   not   he will catch us in   doing nothing

aut in   re   mala. Audiat,   si velit,   nostrum
or in something bad Let (him) hear if he wants   our

colloquium.
discussion

— **Optime loqueris. Secedamus aliquo in**
Very well you speak Let us go aside somewhere into

angulum, ne quis nos impediat.
a corner that not somebody us may hinder

19

Part IV

XII. LEX   COMMODANDI
12   The law   of lending

— Habesne scalpellum?
Do you have   a penknife

— Habeo.
I have

— Oro te, commoda mihi parumper.
I pray you   lend (it)   to me   a while

— Quando reddes?
When   will you give (it) back?

— Cum primum duas pennas exacuero.
When   first   two   pens   I will have sharpened

— Accipe,   sed   ea   lege,   ut   integrum
Receive it   but   with that   law   that   undamaged
                                  (condition)

reddas.
you give (it) back

— **Ea   conditione   acceptum   intelligo;**
  On that   condition   (that) it is accepted   I understand

etiamsi non addidisses.
 even if   not   you would have added (it)

— **Intelligenti   pauca   sufficiunt.**
  To the understanding few (words)   are sufficient

XIII. CAVE MACULAS!
 13   Beware   stains
       (avoid)

— **Visne   mihi   commodare   tuum**
   Are you willing   to me   to lend   your

Terentium?
(book by) Terentius

— **Volo   equidem,   modum   illum   repetas**
  I am willing   indeed   the manner   it   you request back
                        (provided)

 a Conrado,   cui   utendum dedi.
 from   Conrad   to whom   to be used I have given (it)

— Quo signo vis repetam?
By which token you want that I request it back

— Nempe hoc, quod eius habeo Epistolas.
Of course this that his I have Letters

— Id mihi satis est.
That for me enough is

— Sed quando reddes?
But when will you give it back

— Cum descripsero contextum in tres aut
When I will have (it) written out all together in three or

quatuor praelectiones.
four lessons

— Matura igitur, ne meo studio incomodes.
Make haste then that not my study you impede

— Maturabo.
I will make haste

— Sed heus tu, cave macules; alioquin aegre
But hey you beware of stains otherwise reluctantly

commodabo posthac.
I will lend out   after this

— Nempe indignus essem beneficio.
For sure   not worthy I would be of the kindness
{ben5}

XIV. REPETERE PRAELECTIONEM CUM SOCIO
14   To repeat   the lesson   with   a companion

—   Visne   mecum repetere praelectionem?
Do you want   with me   to repeat   the lesson

— Volo.
I want

— Tenesne?
Do you keep it
(know it)

— Non satis recte, fortasse.
Not   enough accurate   maybe

—   Age,   faciamus periculum.
Come on let us make   a try

— Quid igitur exspectamus?
What   then   do we wait for

— Ubi   voles,   incipe.
Where you want   begin
(When)

— Atqui tuum est potius incipere.
But   yours it is rather   to begin

— Quid ita?
What   so
(Why)

— Quia   me invitasti.
Because   me   you have invited

— Aequum dicis.
Fair   you speak

— Attende igitur.
Mind   then

— Istic sum.
Here   I am

XV.   DE   FACIENDO   PERICULO
15   About   making   a try

— Non   decet   hic   otiari   aut garrire, dum
Not   it becomes here to do nothing or   talk   while

praeceptor exspectatur.
the teacher   is expected

— Quid ais?
What do you say?

— Non decet.
Not   it becomes

—   Imo   vero   non   licet,   nisi   volumus
      Nay   indeed   not   it is allowed   unless   we want

vapulare.
to get beaten

—   Tu   igitur,   audi   me   dum   praelectionem
      You   then   hear   me   while   the lesson
                        (listen to)

pronuntio. Ego deinde te audiam.
I pronounce   I   afterwards you will listen to

—   Age,   pronuntia.
     Come on   pronounce

— Nonne teneo?
     Not   do I know (it)

— Nondum recte satis, relege, semel atque
   Not yet correct enough read again one time and

iterum.
again

— Faciam ita.
   I will do so

— Tenesne nunc?
   Do you know (it) now

— Opinor sic; faciam periculum, si vis
   I guess so I will make a try if you are willing

audire me.
to listen to me

— Age, pronuntia. Reddisti omnia recte.
   Come on pronounce (it) You have rendered everything correct

XVI. QUAE PLACET, CULINA AUT SCHOLA?
  16 Which pleases (more) the kitchen or the school

— Unde veniebas modo?
   From where you came just

— E   culina.
From the kitchen

— Quid illuc iveras?
What   thereto did you go for

— Ut   me   calefacerem.
That   me   I would warm
      (myself)

— Tu, credo, libentius   es   in   culina,   quam in
You   I believe   rather   you are in the kitchen than   in
        (prefer to)

schola, nonne?
the school is it not?

— Nihil   mirum: in   schola   non   est   ignis,
  Nothing   surprising   in   the school   not   there is   a fire

sicut in culina.
such as in   the kitchen

— Abi,   sapis.
Go away you are wise

— Utinam   tam saperem in divinis rebus quam
If only (I were) so I were wise in godly   things   as
        (as)

in cura corporis.
in the care of the body

— Fac sapias.
Make that you be wise

— Quomodo?
In which way

— Studio, cura, labore, et diligentia.
By study care effort and diligence

— Non parco labori.
Not I do spare effort

— Recte facis: sed est tempus exspectandum,
Right you do but is time to be awaited

cuius progressu fiunt omnia; interea est
of which by the progress are done all things in the meantime is

precandus Deus assidue.
to be prayed God continually

— Bene mones: utinam illa studia nostra
Well you advise would that those studies our

promoveat in gloriam sui nominis.
He advances to the glory of His name

— Id faciet, si pergamus eum colere
That He will do if we go on Him to worship

diligenter.
diligently

Part V

XVII. QUOMODO LUDAM SINE COLLUSORES?
17   How   may I play   without   playmates

—   Unde   venis?
From where   do you come

— Venio inferne.
I come   from below

— Quod erat tibi negotium infra?
What   was   to you   business   below
           you had

— Iveram redditum urinam.
I went   to make   water
      urinate

—   Sede   nunc   ad   mensam,   et   mane   in
Be seated   now   at   the table   and   remain   in

cubicolo   donec   rediero.
the study cabin   until   I will have come back

— Quid agam interea?
  What   may I do in the meantime

— Edisce praelectionem in diem crastinum, ut
  Learn   the lesson   to the day of tomorrow so that
                       (for)

eam mihi reddas ante coenam.
 it to me you may render before supper

— Iam edidici, praeceptor!
  Already I have learnt (it) by heart   teacher

— Lude igitur.
  Play   then

— Sed nullos habeo collusores.
  But   no   I have   playmates

— Satis multos invenies in hac vicinia, ex
  Enough   many   you will find in this neighbourhood out of

tuis etiam condiscipulis.
your also   fellow pupils

— Nihil id curo nunc: malim (si
  Nothing that I care for now I would like more (if
  (Not at all)

placet	tibi)	ediscere	de	Catechismo	in
it pleases	you)	to learn by heart	from	the Catechism	to (for)

diem Dominicum.

day   the Lords
Sunday

— Ut libet.

   As it pleases (you)

— Si quis te quaeret, quid illi dicam?

   If somebody you   asks for   what to him shall I say

— Dic me prodiisse, sed mox reversurum.

   Say me   to have gone out but soon am to come back
            that I have gone out

XVIII. DE PYRIS INLICITIS

18   About   pears   illegal

— Unde venis?

From where do you come

— A foro.

From the market

— Quis te illuc miserat?

  Who you there   had sent

— Mater.
Mother

— Quid egisti in foro?
What did you do in the market

— Emi pyra.
I have bought pears

— Nescis nobis vetitum esse emere fructus
Don't you know to us forbidden to be to buy fruits

aliquos?
any

— Quis istud ignorat? nam dictum est
Who that does not know for has been said is
(has been)

palam in aula.
publicly in the hall

— Qui igitur ausus es emere pyra?
Who then dared you are to buy pears
(have)

— Mater dederat mihi sextantem, ut mihi
Mother had given to me a sextant that for my(self)

emerem   in   merendam.   Quid   mali
I would buy (something)   to   my afternoon snack   What   of evil
                          (for)   (evil)

  feci,   si   parui   matri?
have I done   if   I obeyed   (my) mother

XIX. AD TONSOREM
19   At   the barber

— Praeceptor,   licetne   nobis   ire   ad   tonsorem?
   Teacher   is it allowed   for us   to go   to   the barber
                              are we allowed

— Quid eo?
   Why   to him

— Ut   capillum   tondeamus.
   That   (our) hair   we shave

— Libenter   quotidie   exiretis   sexies.   Quin
   Gladly   each day   you would go out   six times   Why not
                              {pf}

expectate   in   crastinum   diem,   ut   eatis   una
do you wait   until   of tomorrow   the day   that   you may go   together

cum   caeteris.
with   the others

— Atqui propter forum turba erit in
  But becauise of the market a crowd there will be in

tonstrina.
the barber shop

— Quid tum? satis habebitis otii ad
  What then enough you people will have leasure to
  What does it matter

expectandum. Recipite vos ad studium.
  wait Apply you(rself) to (your) study

— Ut libet, praeceptor.
  As it pleases teacher

XX. PANIS MUTUUM SUMPTUS
20 Bread taken in loan

— Restatne tibi multum panis?
  Remains for you much bread
  Have you left

— Satis, gratia Deo.
  Enough thank (be) to God

— Visne mihi dare mutuo?
  Do you want to me to give (some) in loan

— Libenter.
With pleasure

— Sed fortasse tibi   non sufficiet.
But   maybe   for you   not   there will be enough

—   Imo,   ut spero.
On the contrary as   I hope

— Ad quod usque tempus?
to   what   until   time
      Until what

— Ad diem Veneris.
Until   day   of Venus

—   Unde   habebis   postea?
From where you will have (it) afterwards

— Domo.
From home

— Quis afferet?
Who   will bring (it)

— Egomet ibo   petitum.
I myself   will go to fetch (it)

— Quando?
    When

—   Ipso   die Veneris.
  On the same day   of Venus

— Da mihi mutuo sesquilibram.
  Give to me   in loan   a pound and a half

— Quis appendet?
  Who   will weigh it out

— Uxor   praeceptoris, aut ancilla.
  The wife   of the teacher   or   the woman servant

— Eamus petitum   ex   arca mea.
  Let us go to fetch (it) from   chest   my

—   Quin   ito   solus;   ego   te   in   culina
   Why not   go   by yourself   I   you   in   the kitchen
   (but)

exspectabo.
  will expect

XXI. DE   EPISTULA PATRIS
  21   About   letter   father's

— Quid legis?
  What   do you read

— Literas.
   A letter

—   A   quo?
  From whom

—   A   patre.
  From (my) father

— Quando accepisti?
   When   have you received (it)

—   Heri   vesperi.
  Yesterday   evening

— Quis attulit?
   Who   has brought it

— Nescio.
  I do not know

—   Nescis?   quis tibi reddit eas?
  Don't you know Who to you delivered them
                                            (it)

— Ancilla quaedam a caupone.
Servant some from the innkeeper

— Unde sunt datae?
From where are they dated
(is it)

— Lutetia, credo.
From Paris I believe

— Quo die?
On which day

— Nondum licuit inspicere.
Not yet was (I) allowed to look into (it)

— Nempe ego te interpellavi.
Really I you have interrupted

— Parum refert; non adeo sum occupatus.
Not much it does matter not so I am busy
(that)

— Age: perlege tuam epistolam. Ego interea
Go ahead read you letter I in the meantime

studebo.
will study

39

— Ego quoque mox idem faciam.
   I   too   soon the same wil do

Part VI

XXII. DE DISCIPULO NEGLIGENTE
22   About   the pupil   careless

— Vidistine   librum   meum?
Have you seen   book   my

— Quem   librum   quaeris?
Which   book   do you look for

— Ciceronis Epistolas.
of Cicero   the Letters

— Ubi   reliqueras?
Where   had you left (it)

— Oblitus   eram   in   auditorio.
Forgotten   i was it   in   the auditory
            (had it)

— Tua fuit   negligentia.
Your   it has been   carelessness
That has been your carelessness

41

— Fateor, sed interim indica, si scias
　I confess　but　in the meantime　tell (me)　if　you know

quem accepisse.
whom　to have taken (it)
who has taken it

— Cur non adis praeceptorem? Solet enim
　Why　not　go to　the teacher　　He is accustomed　for

(ut scis) quae a nobis relicta sunt,
(as　you know)　(the things) which　by　us　left　are

aut ferre in museolum, aut alicui dare,
either　to bring　into　(his) study　or　to somebody　to give

qui reddat.
that he　gives (them) back

— Bene mones. O me obliviosum, cui istud in
　Well　you advise　O　me　forgetful　to whom　this　in

mentem non venerat!
mind　not　had come

XXIII. DE TEMPESTATE
　23　About　the weather

—   Unde   redis?
From where   do you come back

— Foris.
From outside

— Cur exieras?
Why   have you gone out

— Redditum urinam.
To give back   urine
To urinate

— Qualis est   coeli   facies?
How   is   of the sky   the aspect

— Nebulosa.
Cloudy

—   An   regelat?
Does it   thaw

— Sic   resolvitur   gelu,   ut   nives   omnino
So   is dispelled   the frost   so that   the snows   wholly
                                                       {nix1pl}

liquescant.
melt

43

— Etiamne pluit?
 Also   does it rain

— Sensi   aliquid   superne   distillare.
 I have felt something from above trickle down

— Fortasse in transitu,   e   stillicidio tecti.
 Perhaps   in passing by from the dripping of the roof

—   Imo   e   nubibus, scio,   quod   si   non
 No, for sure from   the clouds I know   what   if   not
                                       (and that)

  credis,   vide tu ipse.
 you do believe see you yourself
                     (for)

— Quasi ego tibi non   credam   in   re   tantilla.
 As if   I   you   not   would believe in a matter so small

— Cur igitur   dubitare   videbaris?
 Why   then   to be in doubt you seemed

—   Ut   pluribus verbis tecum fabularer.
 In order that with more   words   with you I would talk

— Quorsum id pertinet?
 To what end that   serves

— Ad Latinum sermonem exercendum.
To the Latin language exercising

— Sed interim saepe otiosa verba dicimus;
But in the meantime often idle words we speak

a quibus omnino abstinendum Christus
from which altogether to abstain Christ

praecepit.
has commanded

— Tota erras via in praecepti
In all you are mistaken way in of the commandment
You are completely mistaken

intellectu.
the understanding

— Cur istud dicis?
Why that do you say

— Quia "Non est otiosus sermo, qui ad aliquam
Because "not (it) is idle talk which to some

institutionem refertur', praesertim ubi agitur
instruction refers" especially where the matter is
(when)

de   bonis   et   honestis,   qualia   sunt   Dei   opera   in
about good   and   honest   such as   are   God's works   in

rebus   naturalibus.
matters   natural

— Videris mihi recte sentire; proinde facile   tibi
  You seem to me right to feel   therefore easily with you

assentior.
  I agree

— Sed   haec   hactenus;   instat   nobis   aliud
  But   this   for now   is at hand for us   another
          (so much)   we face

negotium.
  business

— Age,   desinamus.
  Come on   let us stop

XXIV. CHARTAE PRETIUM
  24   Of paper   the price

— A   quo   emisti   istam chartam? —   A
  From whom have you bought   that   paper   From

Fatino.
Fatinus

— Estne bona? — Melior quam ista tua, ut opinor.
Is it good? Better than that yours as I guess

— Nihil miror. — Cur istud dicis?
Nothing I wonder Why that do you say
(Not at all)

— Quia fortasse carior. — Nescio
Because perhaps (it is) more expensive I don't know

— Quanti emisti scapum? — Solido
(For) how much have you bought the quire For a penny

et semisse; tu vero quanti?
and a half (penny) you but (for) how much

— Solido et pluris. — Quanti igitur?
(for) a penny and several How much then

— Quinque quadrantibuas. — Non male profecto
Five farthings Not bad actually

emisti.
you have bought

—   Quinetiam   mercator   dedit   mihi
      Moreover   the merchant   has given   me

auctarium.   — Quodnam, quaeso?
something in addition   What then   I pray (you)

— Schedam chartae bibulae. — O me imprudentem,
   A sheet   of paper   blotting   O   me   fool
                                    what a fool I was

qui oblitus sum petere!
who forgotten are to ask (for it)
        (have)

— Ego ne petivi quidem, sed ultro ille
    I   not   have asked   even   but   unasked   he

dedit: "et hoc (inquit) addo tibi ut me
has given (it)   and   this   he said   I add   for you   that   me

revisas".   —   Sic   solent
you come see again   In this way   they are accustomed

emptores allicere.
  buyers   to entice

— Nec mirum: suum quisque commodum
   And not   surprising   his own   each   advantage

quaerit. — Sed quid agimus, hodierni pensi
seeks   But   what   are we doing   for today   (our) homework

immemores?
not remembering

— Exiguum est; satis temporis nobis restat.
A little bit   it is   enough   time   to us   remains

XXV. DE MUTUO DETRAHENDO
25   About   over a loan   haggling

— Potesne mihi mutuo dare aliquantum pecuniae?
Can you   to me   in loan   give   some   money

— Quantum petis?
How much   you ask

— Quinque asses, si tibi est commodum.
Five   pennies   if   to you   it is   convenient

— Non tot habeo.
Not   so much   I have

— Quot igitur?
How much   then

— Tantum quatuor.
    Only   four

— Bene sane, da mihi istos quatuor.
    Well   quite   give   me   those   four

—   Dabo   dimidium, si vis.
    I will give   half   if you want

— Cur non totum?
    Why not   all

—   Quia sunt mihi opus duo.
    Because   are   to me need   two
                  I have need of

— Da igitur duos, quaeso.
    Give   so   two   I pray

— Sed tibi non sufficient.
    But to you not   they will be sufficient

— Petam ab aliquo alio.
    I will ask from somebody else

—   Accipe   igitur   hos   duos.   Quando
    Receive   so   these   two   When

reddes?
will you give (them) back

— **Die** **Saturni,** **ut** **spero,** **cum** **pater** **ad**
On the day of Saturnus as I hope when (my) father to
On Saturday

forum **venerit.**
the market will have come

— **Esto** **igitur memor.**
  Be then remembering
Do not forget it Do not forget it

— **Ne** **timeas.**
Do not fear

XXVI. DE REDDENDA REGULA
26 About to be given back the ruler

— **Quid** **fecisti** **de** **regula mea?**
What have you done about ruler my
(with)

— **Reliqui** **in** **pergula** **superiore.**
I have left (it) in lecture room upper

— **Cur eam reliquisti?**
Why it you have left

— Oblitus   sum.
Forgotten (it)   I am
            (have)

— Non   recte   factum;   sed   tu   sic   fere
Not   correctly   done   but   you   so   generally

soles,   si   quid   tibi   fuerit   commodatum.
are used (to do)   if   something   to you   has been   lent

— Piget   me   negligentiae   meae.
I feel sorry   me   of neglicence   my
    I feel sorry

— Non   satis   est   dolere,   nisi   mores   mutare
Not   enough   is (it)   to deplore   unless   (your) ways   to change

velis.
you are willing

— Deum   precabor,   ut   mihi   mutare   velit.
God   I will pray   that   me   change   He wills

— Si   sapis;   alioqui   nemo   tibi   posthac
If   you are wise   otherwise   nobody   to you   after this

commodare   volet.
to lend   will be willing

— Habeo gratiam, quod me tam amice
　I have　thanks　because　me　so　friendly
　I am grateful

monueris.
you have warned

— I nunc petitum meam regulam; est enim ea
　Go now to fetch my ruler is for it

mihi opus ad ducendas in charta lineas.
to me need to draw in the paper lines
　　　　　　　　　　　(on)

— Nunc eo.
　Now I go

— Refer ad me in cubiculum.
　Bring (it) back to me to my study cabin

— Mox habebis.
　Soon you will have (it)

Part VII

XXVII. PRAECEPTOR LIBERALIS
27   The teacher   generous

—   Praeceptor,   visne   mihi   mutuo   dare
     Teacher   are you willing   to me   in loan   to give

aliquantulum pecuniae?
a small amount   of money

— Quid opus est   tibi   pecunia?
    What   need   is there   to you   (for) money
    Why do you need money

—   Ut   Sylvio   satisfaciam.
    That   to Sylvius   I pay my debt

— Quantum   debes   illi?
    Hiow much   do you owe   to him

—   Assem   cum   semisse.
    One penny   with   a half
           (and)

— Quo   nomine?
 By what   name
       (debt)

— Quia   scripsit   mihi aliquot colloquia.
 Because he has written for me   some   colloquia
        (copied out)

— Ostende.
  Let see

— Vide, si placet.
  See   if it pleases
        please

— Adi   hypodidascalum, dic   ut   det   quantum
 Go to   the undermaster   say   that he gives   as much as
                                              {coni}

petis.
you ask

— Gratias   ago,   praeceptor.
 Thanks   I bring on   teacher
       Thank you

— Non est quod   agas;   sed refer in
 Not   it is   that   you you must say thanks but   report into
                                                (enter it)

codicem   tuum.
account book   your

— Quin   iam   retuli.
For sure already I have entered (it)

— Factum bene, ostende   ipsi   hypodidascalo.
Done   well   show   to the same   undermaster

XXVIII. PASTINARE VITES
28   To weed   the vines

— Ubi   fuisti   his   diebus?
Where have you been in these   days

— Ruri.
In the countryside

— Quo in loco?
Which in   place

— In villa nostra.
In   estate   our

— Quid agebas illic?
What did you do there

— Ministrabam patri.
I helped   (my) father

— Quid vero ille?
What   but   (did) he

— Pastinabat vites nostras.
He weeded   vines   our

— Quando   illinc   rediisti?
When   from there you have come back

—   Heri   tantum.
Yesterday   only

—   Quid   pater?
What (about) (your) father

—   Una   mecum reversus est.
Together with me returned he is
                            (has)

— Bene factum. Sed quo nunc is?
Well   done   But where now you go

— Recta domum.
Straight   home

— Quando   repetes   ludum literarium?
When   will you go again to the play   literary
                          school

—   Cras,   iuvante   Deo,   aut   summum
         Tomorrow   helping   God   or   at most

perendie.
the day after tomorrow

— Ergo   interim   vale.
    Then   in the meantime   goodbye

— Et tu   interim   vale,   mi Francisce.
   And   you   in the meantime   goodbye   my   Franciscus

XXIX. PATER ABIENS PECUNIAM DAT
   29   The father   going away   money   gives

—   Abiit   tuus pater?
   Has gone away   your   father

— Abiit.
   He has gone away

—   Quota   hora?
   At how many   hour
     (which)

— Prima   pomeridiana.
   The first   of the afternoon

— Quid   dixit   tibi?
What   has he said to you

—   Multis   verbis   monuit   me   ut   diligenter
    With many   words   he has advised   me   that   assiduously

studerem.
I should study

— Utinam sic facias.
    May   so   you do

— Faciam, Deo iuvante.
   I will do   God   helping

—   Ecquid   pecuniam   dedit   tibi?
   {question marker}   money   he has given to you

—   Dedit,   ut fere   solet.
   He has given as generally he is used (to do)

— Quantum?
   How much

— Nihil ad te.
   None to you
   None of your business

— Fateor; sed tamen quid facies ista
I confess but nevertheless what will you do with that

pecunia?
money

— Emam chartam, et alia quae mihi sunt
I will buy paper and other things which to me are

usui.
for use
(useful)

— Quod si amiseris?
What if you have lost (it)

— Aequo animo ferendum erat.
With a calm mind to be borne it was
with equanimity

— Quid si forte eguero, dabisne mutuo?
What if maybe I will have need will you give in loan
{pf}

— Dabo et quidem libenter.
I will give and even with pleasure

— Habeo tibi gratiam.
I have to you grace
I am grateful to you

XXX. NON LICET MANERE DOMI
30   Not   it is allowed to remain at home

— Quid ita es laetus?
What so are you happy
(Why)

— Quia venit pater.
Because has come father

— Ain' tu? Unde venit?
Say you from where has he come
Really?

— Lutetia.
From Lutetia
{Paris}

— Quando advenit?
When has he arrived

— Modo.
Just now

— Iamne salutavisti?
Already have you greeted (him)

— Salutavi cum ex equo descenderit.
I have greeted (him) when off (his) horse he had descended

— Quid amplius illi fecisti?
What further for him you have done

— Calcaria detraxi et ocreas.
(His) spurs I have taken off and (his) boots

— Miror te non mansisse domi propter eius
I wonder you not stayed at home because of his

adventum.
coming

— Nec ille permisisset, nec ego vellem,
Neither he would have permitted (it) nor I would wish

praesertim nunc, cum audienda est praelectio.
especially now when to be heard is the lesson

— Bene tibi consulis, qui
Well for you you take counsel who
Well considered that you

temporis rationem habeas; sed quid pater?
of time reason you have but what of (your) father
take your time in consideration

Valetne?
Is he healthy
(well)

— Recte, Dei beneficio.
Well of God by the blessing

— Equidem gaudeo plurimum, tua et eius
Truly I rejoice very much for your and his

causa, quod salvus peregrine redieret.
sake because safe from abroad he has come back

— Facis ut amicum decet, sed cras pluribus
You do as a friend becomes but tomorrow with more

verbis colloquemur.
words we will talk together

— Vidi praeceptorem, qui iam ingreditur
I have seen the teacher who already enters

auditorium.
the auditory

— Eamus auditum praelectionem.
Let us go to hear the lesson

XXXI. DE OBSONIO
31 About food

63

— Ubi est frater tuus?
Where is brother your

— Modo ivit domum.
Just now he has gone home

— Quid eo?
What to him
What is he going to do

— Petitum nobis obsonium.
To fetch for us food

— Quid nunc opus est vobis obsonio?
Why now need there is to you food
          do you need

— In merendam.
For the afternoon snack

— An non habetis in arca vestra?
{Question marker} not do you have in chest your
                              (container)

— Non.
No

— Quid ita non?
Why so not
Why not

— Quia mater non solet dare nobis
Because mother not is accoustomed to give to us

obsonium, nisi in praesens tempus.
food unless to the present time
(for)

— Nempe quia novit vos esse gulosos.
For sure because she knows you to be gluttonous

— Quomodo gulosi sumus?
In which way gluttonous we are?

— Quia fortasse uno convicto devoratis, quod in
Because perhaps in one meal you devour what for

tres datum fuerit.
three given has been

— Tace, ego dicam praeceptori fratrem tuum
Shut up I will say to the teacher brother your
that your brother does

nihil aliud quam discurrere.
nothing else than to run about

— Atqui non solet prodire, nisi cum
But not he is accustomed to go out unless with

bona   venia   praeceptoris.
the good   permission   of the teacher
    permission

— Atqui   praeceptorem   fallit!
    But   the teacher   he deceives

— Quomodo   fallit   eum?
    How   does he deceive   him?

—   Non   enim   mens   est   praeceptoris,   ut
     not   Because   the mind   it is   of the teacher   that
                 (intention)

ter   quotidie   prodeat.
three times   each day   he should go out

—   Sine   illum   venire;   videbis   quid   tibi
     Let   him   come   you will see   what   to you

respondeat.
he will answer

—   Imo   videat   quid   praeceptori
     On the contrary   let (him) see   what   to the teacher

respondeat.
he may answer

XXXII.   AS   VALET LIBRUM
32   A penny is worth   a book

— Quantum habes pecuniae?
How much   you have   of money
(money)

— Assem cum semisse. Quantum habes tu?
A penny   with   a half   How much   do have you
(and)

— Non tantum.
Not   that much

— Quantum igitur?
How much   then

— Unicum assem.
Just one   penny

—   Vis   dare   mutuo?
Will you give (it)   in loan
lend it

— Est mihi opus.
It is for me   need
I need it

— In quem usum?
To   what   use
(for)

— Ad emendam chartam.
    To to be bought   paper
   To buy paper

— Hodie   reddam   tibi.
   Today   I will give (it) back to you

—   Addendum   fuit: Deo iuvante.
   There should be added have been God   helping

— Sic praeceptor docet e   verbo Dei, sed non
  So   the teacher   teaches from the word of God but   not

possum assuescere.
  I can   get used (to it)

— Fac assuescas.
  Make that you get used

— Quomodo id fiet?
  In which way that shall be done?

— Si saepe cogites,   nos   a Deo sic pendere,
  If   often   you consider (that) we from God so   depend
                                     (on)

ut nihil possimus facere sine eius auxilio.
that nothing we can   do   without His   help

— Bonum mihi das consilium.
A good   to me   you give   advice

— Quale mihi dare velim.
Such as   to me   to give   I would want
       (to myself)

— Sed (ut ad propositum redeamus), dabis
But   (that   to   the purpose   we may return)   will you give
     (subject)

mutuo istum assem?
in loan   that   penny

— Miror te mutuo petere qui habes
I wonder   (that) you   in loan   ask   (you) who   you have

plus quam ego.
more   than   I

— Est quidam scholasticus hac transiens, qui
There is   some   scholar   this way   passing by   who

librum venalem ostentat.
a book   for sale   offers

— Quid tum? — Cupiebam emere, quia vilius
what   So   I wished   to buy (it)   because   cheaper

indicat   quam   noster   bibliopola.
he puts a price   than   our   bookseller

—   Accipe: sed,   quaeso,   unde   tam   cito
       Take it   but   I ask   from where   so   quickly
                                                    (soon)

reddes?
you will give (it) back

—   A   coena   ibo   domum,   ut   a   matre
      From   dinner   I will go   home   that   from   (my) mother
      (After)

petam.
  I ask

—   Quid,   si   dare   nolit?
     What   if   to give   she is not willing

—   Not   cunctabitur,   cum   librum   ostendero.
     Not   she will hesitate   when   the book   I shall have shown

Part VIII

XXXIII. FAMULUS SCRIPSIT LITERAS
33   The manservant has written the letter

— Quid sibi vult, quod   abfueris   hac tota
What to itself it will   that   you have been absent this whole
What does it mean

hebdomade?
week
{hebdomas5}

— Oportuit   me manere domi.
It was proper for me   to stay   at home
        I had to

— Quamobrem?
For what reason

— Ut   matri   adessem, quae aegrotabat.
That by (my) mother I would be   who   was ill

— Quod illi officium praestabas?
What to her service   you rendered

— Saepius   ei   legebam.
mMore often to her   I read
(rather often)

— Quod legebas?
What   did you read

— Aliquid   ex   sacris   litteris.
Something from the Holy Scriptures

— Sanctum   istud   et   laudabile   ministerium.
A holy   that   and   praiseworthy   ministry

Utinam   sic   omnes   studerent   verbo   Dei.   Sed
Would that so   all   would study the word of God But

quid? Nihil   agebas   praeterea?
what   nothing Did you do   besides

— Quoties   opus   erat,   illi   ministrabam
As often as   need   there was   her   I served
                       needed

cum   ancilla.
together with a woman servant

— Suntne   haec   vera?
Are   these things   true

— Habeo testimonium.
   I have   a testimony

— Profer illud.
   Bring out   it

— Ecce!
   See
 (Here it is)

— Quis scripsit?
   Who   has written (it)

— Famulus noster, matris nomine.
   manservant   our   mothers' in name

— Agnosco eius   manum,   quia   saepe   ab   illo
   I recognize his   hand(writing) because often   from him

mihi attulisti.
 me   you have brought (a letter) to

— Licetne igitur redire in sedem meam?
   Is it allowed   so   to go back to   seat   my

— Quidni   liceat,   cum mihi satisfeceris?
   How not it is allowed while   me   you have satisfied

— Gratias ago, Praeceptor!
Thanks I bring teacher!
Thank you

XXXIV. FAMULI QUIDEM LATINE FABULANTUR
34 The manservants even in Latin talk

— Quot annos habes?
How many years you have
(are)

— Tredecim, ut a matre accepi. Tu vero?
Thirteen as from mother I received (word) you But

— Equidem non tot habeo.
Sure not so many I have
(am)

— Quot igitur?
How many then

— Deest unus.
is lacking one

— Sunt ergo duodecim.
They are so twelve

— In promptu est ratio.
in sight is calculation
That is an obvious

— Sed frater tuus quotum agit annum?
But brother your how-muchest he does year
in what year is he

— Quintum.
The fifth

— Quid ais? Iam Latine loquitur.
What do you say Already in Latin he speaks

— Quid miraris? Semper habemus domi
Why do you wonder Always we have at home

paedagogum et doctum et diligentem: is semper
a paedagogue both learned and diligent he always

nos Latine loqui docet; nihil Anglicum effert,
us in Latin to speak teaches nothing English he brings out

nisi aliquid declarandi causa: quin etiam
unless something explaining for the sake of nay even

patrem non audemus nisi Latine alloqui.
father not we hear if not in Latin speak to (us)

— Nunquam igitur Anglice loquimini?
Never so in English you speak
So you never speak in English

— Solum cum matre, idque certa quadam hora,
Only with mother and that fixed on some hour

cum illa nos ad se vocari iubet.
when she us to herself to be called orders

— Quid agitis cum familia?
What do you do with the (people of) the household

— Cum familia rarus est nobis sermo, et
With the household seldom is for us word and
we speak

quidem tantum in transitu; et tamen
even (that) only in passing and nevertheless

famuli ipsi nos Latine alloquuntur.
the manservants themselves us in Latin speak to
(even)

— Quid ancillae?
What about the woman servants

— Si quando usus postulat ut eas
If at some moment custom requests that them

alloquamur, utimur sermone vernaculo, ut
we speak to we use language indigenous as
the vernacular

76

solemus cum ipsa matre.
we are accustomed   with   herself   mother

— O vos felices, qui tam diligenter
O   you   lucky people   (you) who   so   carefully

docemini!
are taught

— Est Deo gratia, cuius dono patrem habemus
is   to God   thanks   whose   by gift   a father   we have

qui curet nos tam accurate erudiendos.
who   takes care   (that) we   so   painstakingly   must be educated

— Certe eius rei laus et honor unico coelesti
Surely   of this   matter   praise   and   honour   alone   heavenly

Patri debetur.
the Father   is owed to

— Sed quid agimus? Iam audio recitari
But   what   do we do   Already   I hear   be read aloud

catalogos.
the rolls

— Ergo festinemus.
  So   let us hurry

XXXV. CLYSTERES MALARIAE REMEDIUM
  35   Clysters   to malaria   a remedy

— Quid   egisti   per   hos   quindecim   dies?
  What   have you done during these   fifteen   days
        {pf ago}   two weeks

— Ministravi matri, quae graviter aegrotabat.
  I have served mother   who   seriously   was ill

— Ain'   tu?
  Do say   you
  Really?

— Sic est profecto.
  so   it is   Sure

— Quo laborabat morbo?
  Which   she suffered   illness

— Febre tertiana.
  Fever   tertian
  {febris5}

—   An   convaluit?
          If   has she recovered
  question marker)

— Paulatim convalescit, gratia Deo.
Little by little   she recovers   thanks   to God

— Quis eam sanavit?
Who   her   has healed

— Medicorum summus.
of the doctors   the highest

— Quis ille?
Who   is he

— Ipse Deus.
Himself   God

— De hoc nihil dubito. Sed cuius opera?
About   that   nothing   I doubt   But   by whose   work
          (not at all)

Deus sanat, medicus curat.
God   heals   the doctor   cures

— Domini Sarasini.
Mr.   Sarasinus'

— Is habetur maximi nominis in
That man   is held   of the greatest   name   in
          is of the greatest renown

Medicinae professione.
of medicine   the profession
   medical

— **Id quotidie probant egregiae curationes eius.**
  That   daily   prove   excellent   treatments   his

—   **Quibus**   **remediis**   **utebatur**
          Which   remedies   did he use

in curanda matre tua?
in to be treated mother your
in the treatment of your mother

— **Medicamentis.**
      Medicines

— **Satis istud intelligo, etiam te tacente. Sed**
  enough   that I understand   also you not saying (it) But
                            also when you do not tell

dic plane, quae fuerunt ista medicamenta?
say plainly which have been those   medicines

— **Sine me aliquantisper recordari.**
  Let   me   for a while   remember
                     (recollect)

— **Sino; dic tandem quae reminisceris.**
   I let (you) say   at last   what you remember

— Duo tantum nomina mihi occurrunt, Clysteres
  Two   only   names to me occur   clysters

et Potiones.
and potions

— Quid ista conferunt?
  What these did avail

— Eho inepte, ita rogas, quasi ego medicinae
  Hey you silly thus you ask as if I to medicine

operam dederim. Itaque si cupis amplius scire,
  work I have given Therefore if you wish wider to know
I have applied myself to   (more)

quaere tute ipse ab iis potius qui ita
  ask safely yourself from those rather who so

profitentur, hoc est, a medicis et
profess (to do) that is from the doctors and

pharmacopolis.
  the pharmacists

— Ne mihi succenseas, oro.
  Do not to me be angry I pray

— Cur tu es adeo curiosus?
Why you are so curious

— Ut ediscam semper aliquid.
In order that I learn always something

— At vide interim ne voceris
But see in the meantime that not you are called

percontator.
an inquisitive fellow

— Audi tamen item pauca.
Hear however as well a few things

— Loquere.
Speak

— Quamdiu aegrotavit mater?
How long has been ill (your) mother

— Fere duas hebdomadas.
About two weeks

— Interea ubi erat pater?
In the meantime where was (your) father

— Profectus erat Lugdunum ad mercatum.
Left   he was   to Lyon   to   the market
         (had)

— Sed   tu,   qua   hora   rediisti   in
But   you   at which   time   have you come back   to

Gymnasium?
the gymnasium

— Hodie mane.
Today   early

— Dedistine excusationem praeceptori?
Did you give   excuse   to the teacher
         Have you apologized

— Dedi.
I have given

— Quid tibi respondit?
What   to you   he has answered

— Factum bene inquit. Tu vero ubi eras?
Done   well   he said   You   but   where   you were

— Hesterno   die   rus   iveram   cum
Of yesterday   the day   to the contryside   I had gone   with
         Yesterday

patruo.
(my) uncle

— Age, videamus quid simus reddituri hora
Come on let us see what we are to render hour

secunda; nam ego quodammodo nunc novus sum
in the second for I in some way now a new am

discipulus.
pupil

XXXVI. LAVANTUR DENTES, NON VESTIMENTA
36 Are washed the teeth not the clothes

— Demiror tuam negligentiam.
I wonder at your negligence

— Qua in re tandem?
which in matter then

— Quod te non curas diligentius.
That you not you care for more diligently
(yourself)

— Ego vero me curo fortasse nimis. Satis
I but me take care for maybe too much Enough
(myself)

edo, bibo, dormio, quae est Dei erga me
I eat I drink I sleep which is God's towards me

benignitas. Praeterea pecto capillum, lavo manus,
kindness furthermore I comb (my) hair I wash (my) hands {manus1pl}

faciem, dentes, oculos, et haec mane
face teeth eyes and these things in the morning

praecipue. Quinetiam, cum tempus postulat, corpus
especially Moreover when the time (moment) requires (it) the body

exerceo, relaxo animum, et ludo cum caeteris.
I exercise I relax the mind and I play with the others

Quid vis amplius?
What do you want further

— Mittamus ista: non ea sunt quae
Let we send (Let go) those things not those are (the things) which

in te reprehendo.
in you I reproach

— Quid igitur?
What then

— Circumspice vestimenta tua
　 Look about　　　clothes　　your

a calce ad verticem. Nihil integrum invenies,
from heel to top　 Nothing whole you will find
　 from top to toe

omnia sunt lacera et obsoleta. Ista profecto
all are torn and worn out Those things indeed

nequaquam vestrum genus decent. Si saltem
in no way　　 your　 kind adorn If at least
　　　　　　　　 (family)

curares vestitum tuum sarciendum, aut
you would take care of your clothing your to be mended or

quoque modo instaurandum.
in some way to be repaired

— Loqueris tu quidem quae libent.
　 Talk you just the things which please (to you)

Quod si parentes haberes tam procul remotos,
Because if parents you would have so far distant

fortasse non esses elegantior. Si mihi pecunia
maybe not you would be more elegant If to me the money

suppeteret,   non   paterer   me   usque   adeo
would be in store   not   I would suffer   me   until   so much
                                       (myself)   to such a degree

pannosum   esse.
dressed in rags   to be

XXXVII. LIBER MUTUUS PIGNORI OPPONITUR
37   A book   on loan   in pledge   is given

— Comoda   mihi   Virgilium   tuum   in   duos   dies,   si
    Lend   to me   Virgil   your   for   two   days   if

nullo   incomodo   tuo   id   fieri   potest.
with no at all   inconvenience   your   that   be done   can
without any inconvenience for you

— Profecto   non   possum.
    Actually   not   I can

— Cur   non?
    Why   not

— Quia   Gerardus,   qui   a   me   commodato
   Because   Gerard   who   from   me   on loan

acceperat,   pignori   opposuit.
it had received   in pledge   it has given

— Ain' tu, pignori?
   Say you in pledge
   Really?

— Sic est,   ut   dico.
   So it is (just) as I say

—   Quanti   oppignaverit?
   For how much he has pledged it

— Tribus (ut   ait)   assibus.
   For three (as he says) pennies

— O, hominem ingratum!
   Oh   person   ungrateful

— Tantumne ingratum?
   Just only   ungrateful

— Imo   vero   et   ingratum,   et   malum.   Sed
   Nay   for sure and   ungrateful and   bad   But
                (both)

nunquid   ille   rem   tuam   oppignorare   potuit,
can it be that the   thing your   plegde   he could
               (property)   {pf}

te inconsulto?
you not consulted
without consulting you

— Potuit, ut factum vides.
He could as has been done you see

— Non tamen debuit
Not however he should
{pf}

— Rem acu tetigisti, sed quid
The thing with a needle you have touched but what
you have hit the nail on the head

facerem?
should I do

— Rogas? Defer eum ad praeceptorem!
You ask Denounce him to the teacher

— Malo istam pati iniuriam, quam
I like more that to suffer injustice than

committere ut miser vapulet.
to bring together that the poor fellow gets a beating
(make) {coni}

— Bene facis, dummodo tuum reddat.
Well you do provided your (property) he gives back

— Reddet, spero.
He will give (it) back I hope

— Unde redderet?
   Whence   will he give (it) back

— Ait,   se   brevi   accepturum   a   patre
   He says   himself   in short   is to receive   from   (his) father

pecuniam.
   money

— Quid si te fallit?
   What   if   you   he deceives

— Fieri   potest,   sed   tamen   aliquot   dies
   Happen   it can   but   nevertheless   several   days
          (may)   (a few)

exspectabo   quid   sit   futurum,   deinde   consilium
   I will wait   what   be   to be   thereafter   a decision
                      (is)

capiam.
   I will take

— Recto   consilio   nihil   est tutius.
   than a right   decision   Nothing   is   safer

— Meministi   probe,   sic   enim   praeceptor
   You remember   well   so   because   the teacher

dictavit   nobis.   Sed   nunquid   vis
has prescribed   to us   But   can it be that   you want

aliud?
(something) else

— Ut   sit   bene   tibi.   Et   tibi,   optime.
   May   it be   well   to you   And   to you   (my) best
                                             (my most dear)

Part IX

XXXVIII. PULVISCULUS IN OCULO SOCII
38   A dust grain   in   the eye   of a comrade

— Obsecro te, Samuel, da mihi operam paulisper.
I beseech you Samuel give me help a little while

— Quid istud est?
What that is
What's the problem

— Nescio quid incidit mihi in oculum, quod
I don't know what has got me into the eye which

me habet valde male.
me has very much badly
hurts me a lot

— In utrum oculum incidit?
Into which eye it has got

— In dextrum.
Into the right (eye)

— Vis   inspiciam?
Do you want that I look into (it)

— Inspice,   amabo   te.
Look into (it)   I will love   you
                (be grateful to)

— Aperi quantum potes: ac tene immobilem.
Open (it) as much as you can and keep   motionless
        (wide as)

— Non queo a nictu continere.
Not I am able from blinking to withhold (myself)

— Mane, egomet tenebo   sinistra manu.
Stay   I   will hold (it) with the left hand

— Ecquid   vides?
Something at all do you see

— Video aliquid minutum.
I see   something   tiny

— Exime (quaeso) si potes.
Take (it) out   (I pray) if you can

— Quin iam exemi.
Actually already I have taken (it) out

— O factum bene! Quid est?
Oh   done   well   What   is it

— Cerne tu ipse.
Look   you yourself

— Est mica pulveris.
It is a grain   of dust

— Et quidem usque adeo pusilla, ut vix cerni
And   even   until   so   tiny   that hardly be seen
             so very

possit.
it can

— Vide quantum doloris adferat oculis res tam
See how much of pain brings to the eyes a thing so
             (pain)

exigua!
small

— Haud mirum quidem. Nullum enim, e
Not (it is) surprising however No one Because out of
                          (of)

membris exterioribus, oculo tenerius esse
the limbs   outer than the eye more tender to be
(parts of the body)

dicitur.   Inde   etiam   fit,   ut   experiamur
is said   From there   also   it happens   that   we find out

nihil   nobis   esse   charius.
nothing   to us   to be   more precious

— Non   mihi   rubet   oculus?
Not   to me   becomes red   the eye

— Aliquantulum, nempe   quia   fricuisti.
A little bit   certainly   because   you have rubbed (it)

— Credin'   tu   mihi adhuc   dolere?
Do believe   you   to me   still   (it) to ache
(it aches)

— Quidni   credam,   qui   toties   talem
How not   I would believe (it)   (I) who   so many times   such

molestiam   sum   expertus?
trouble   I am   experienced
(have)

— Experientia   est   rerum   magistra.
Experience   is   of things   the teacher

— Ita   vulgo   dicitur.
Thus   by the people   it is said

— Quid pretii dabo isti medico pro labore?
  What of price I will give to this doctor for his work
       (price)

— Quantum pacti sumus.
  As much as agreed we are
              (have)

— Brevis est conclusio: ergo nihil. Sed tamen
  Short is the conclusion ergo nothing but nevertheless

habeo tibi gratiam, atque utinam detur
I have to you thanks and would that may be given
  I am grateful to you

referendae locus.
for bringing back place
occasion for returning it

— Quin potius avertat Deus.
  May rather ward (that) off God

— Bene correxisti; dixeram imprudenter, at
  Well you have amended I have spoken rashly but

sine dolo.
without deceit
         (malice)

— Sic accepi, sed interim iocari licet,
  So I have taken (it) but meanwhile to joke it is allowed

praesertim   ut   in   Latina   lingua   nos
especially   in order that   in   the Latin   tongue   ourselves

exerceamus.
we exercise

—   Faxit   Dominus   Deus   ut   omnia   studia   nostra
May grant   the Lord   God   that   all   studies   our

ad   gloriam   ipsius   referantur.
to   glory   His   are related

—   Faxit   precor.
May He grant (it)   I pray

— Bene   correxisti
Well   you have corrected

XXXIX.   DE   CARNE   COLLOQUIUM
39   About   meat   a discussion

— Quid   tibi   dedit   mater   in   merendam?
What   to you   has given   (your) mother   for   your afternoon snack

— Vide.
See

— Caro est, sed quaenam?
Meat   it is   but   what (meat)

— Bubula.
Beef

— Utrum recens an salsa?
Whether   fresh   or   salted

— Est bubula salita.
It is   beef   salted

— Utrum pinguis an macra?
Whether   fat   or   meager
(lean)

— Eho inepte, non vides macram esse?
Ho   you silly (boy)   not   do you se   lean   it to be
that it is lean

— Annon malles esse vitulinam aut
Did not you   like more   (it) to be   veal   or

vervecinam?
mutton

— Utraque bona est, sed in omni genere
Both   good   is   but   in   all   kind
(among)   (kinds)

sapit mihi hoedina, praesertim assa.
is to taste / I like — to me — a young goat's — especially — roasted

— Hem, delicatule, iamne palatum tam doctum
Oh — you little gourmet — already — a palate — so — learned (expert)

habes?
you have

— Dico ut sentio. Non enim est mentiendum.
I say — as — I feel — Not — for — is — to lie / It is forbidden to lie

— Sed ad rem. Suilla quoque vescor libenter,
But — to — the matter — Pork — too — I eat — with pleasure

modico sale aspersa et bene cocta.
with a little — salt — sprinkled — and — well — boiled

— O mirificam Dei gratiam, qui dat nobis
Oh — wonderful — of God — grace — who — gives — to us

tot obsoniorum genera et tam bona!
so many — of foods (of food) — kinds — and — so — good

— Quot putas esse in urbe pauperes qui solo
How many — you think — to be — in — town — poor people — who — alone

pane | hordeaceo | victitant, | neque | tamen | ad
on bread | barley | subsist | and not | nevertheless (even) | to

saturitatem?
repletion

— Non | dubito | multos | esse, | in | tanta | praesertim
Not | I doubt | many | to be | in | such a | especially
| | that there are many

annona | caritate.
of grain | dearth

— Itaque | nos, | in | tanta | bonarum | rerum
Therefore | we | in (amidst) | so great a | of good | things

copia, | quantas | Deo | gratias | agere | debemus, | quas
plenty | how many (much) | to God | thanks | to give | we must | what

laudes | illi | dicere?
praise | to Him | to say

— Eius | igitur | beneficia | magnifice | ubique
His | therefore | gifts | magnificently | everywhere

praedicemus: | atque | interim | precemur, | ut
we proclaim | and | in the meantime | pray {coni} | that

pauperum   suorum misereatur inopiae.
of poor people   His   he has mercy   of the need

— Utinam ipse corda nostra suo Spiritu ad eam
    May   He   hearts   our   by His Spirit   to   that

rem penitus afficiat.
matter   deeply   move

— Ita precor.
   So   I pray

XL. DE RATIONE FRUCTUS EMENDI
40 About the system   fruits   in buying

—   Fuistine   hodie in foro?
  Have you been   today   in   the market

— Fui.
  I have been

— Quando?
    When

— Post concionem sacram.
  After   the meeting   holy
        the church service

— Quid   emisti   nobis?
What   have you bought   for us

— Fere nihil.
Almost nothing

— Quid autem?
What   but

— Butyrum.
Butter

— Quanti?
How much

— Quadrante.
For a farthing
{quadrans5}

— Tantillum?
So little

— Non ausus sum amplius emere.
Not   dared   I am   wider   to buy
              (have)   (more)

— Quid timebas?
What   were you afraid of

— Ne bonum esset.
   Lest   good   it would be

— Satis prudenter factum.
   Enough   cautious   done

— Cur istum dicis, here?
   Why   that   you say master

— Quia malim te esse hac in re timidiorem,
   Because I like more you to be this in matter more fearful
                                           (too fearful)

quam audaciorem. Sed nunquid emisti
than   more bold   But   possibly   you have bought
        (too bold)

praeterea?
besides that

— Nihil.
   Nothing

— Eho! nihilne?
   What?! Nothing?

— Nihil prorsus.
   Nothing   at all

— Vah,   quam   parce   nobis   opsonatus   es!
Phew!   how   frugally   for us   purchased victuals   you are
                                                                        (you have)

— Quid   aliud   emere   potuissem?
What   else   to buy   could I
                              {plqpf}

— Quasi   nescias   quibus   cibis   oblectari   soleam.
As if   you don't know   which   foods   to delight in   I use
                                          (food)

— Scio   te   amare   caseum   molliusculum,   et   pyra,
I know   you   to love   cheese   a bit soft   and   pears
         that you love

et   alios   fructus   recentes.
and   other   fruits   fresh

— Recte   dicis;   cur   ergo   non   emebas?
Correctly   you say   why   then   not   you bought (them)

— Caseus   ipse   carior   erat   pro   nostra
Cheese   that   more expensive   it was   for   our
                  (too expensive)

pecuniola.
little bit of money

— Quid   fructus?
What (about)   the fruits

— Alii erant non satis maturi, de aliis ego
Others were not enough ripe about others I
(Some)

dubitabam essentne boni.
doubted whether they would be good

— Miser, non poteras gustare?
Wretched fellow not could you taste (them)

— Atqui istae mulieres nihil gustare permittunt,
But those women nothing to taste do permit

nisi te empturum affirmes.
unless you will buy you assure
that you are going to buy (it)

— Nihil mirum; multi enim gustarent
Nothing surprising many for taste

animi tantum gratia. Tu igitur
of the mind only by grace You then
because they fancy (it) because they fancy (it)

esto alias prudentior.
be another time more prudent
(clever)

— Quomodo?
In which way

— Si videris pulchrum aliquem fructum, eme
If you have seen fair any fruit buy

aliquantulum denariolo, ut facias
a little quantity just for a little money that you may make

periculum.
a try

— Quid tum praeterea?
What then thereafter

— Si tibi sapuerit, tum emito amplius; sin
If to you it has tasted (good) `then buy wider but if
(more)

minus, relinquito, et alio te conferre.
less leave it alone and elsewhere you(rself) bring on
(not quite) go on

— Bona est ista cautio.
a good is that caution

— Memineris igitur, ut ipse postea
Do you remember then that (your)self afterwards
(henceforth)

utaris.
you use (it)

— Ego, ut spero, meminero diligenter. Nunquid
I as I hope will remember (it) carefully Anything
(so)

vis praeterea?
you want besides

— Ut cures quae tui sunt officii,
That you attend to (the things) which of your are duty

deinde literis incumbas.
then (your) book apply yourself to

XLI. DE PRETIO CARNIS VITULINAE
41 About the price of meat veal

— Unde redis?
From where do you come back

— Foro.
(From) the market

— Quid emisti?
What have you bought

— Carnem.
Meat

— Qualem? — Vitulinam.
  What kind   Veal

— Ostende, quaeso, fere nova res est hoc
  Let see   I pray almost a new thing it is in this

tempore.
  time
(season)

— Vide.
  Look

— Bona videtur mihi.
  Good it seems to me

— Non falleris, opinor.
  Not you are mistaken I guess

— Quot sunt librae?
  How many there are pounds

— Nolunt lanii appendere vitulinam.
  are not willing the butchers to weigh out the veal

— Cur non?
  Why not

— Propter novitatem.
   Because of   the novelty
           (it is new)

— Vide   astutiam: scilicet   quisque   vendit
   See   (their) astuteness   that is   everybody   sells

quam potest carissime.
 which   he can   the most dear
as dear as possible

— Rem   acu   tetigisti.
   The matter with a needle you have touched
   You hit the head on the nail

— Quantum   putas   pendere?
   How much   do you think (it) to weigh

— Duas libras et paulo amplius.
   Two   pounds and a little   wider
                       (more)

— Quanti   emisti?
   Of how much have you bought (it)
   (what for)

— Age,   divina.
   Come on   make a guess

— Non sum divinus.
   Not   I am   soothsayer
          (godly)

— Atqui multi divinant, qui tamen divini
   But   many people make guesses who however soothsayers

non sunt.
not   are

— Fieri potest. Sed ex quibusdam
   Happen it can   But   from   certain
      Maybe   (on the basis of)

coniecturis: alioqui divinatio vetita est in
suppositions   otherwise soothsaying forbidden is in

divinis literis.
the divine   book

— Divina igitur ex coniectura.
   Guess then   from a supposition
         (on the basis of)

— Emisti totum duobus assibus?
   Have you bought the whole for two pennies

— Paulo minoris.
   For a bit   less

— Quanti ergo?
   Of how much then
   For how much

— Tenta iterum.
  Try   again

— Viginti denariolis.
  Twenty   small coins

—   Nolo   te diutius torqueri de nihilo.
  I do not want you still longer torment about nothing

— Dic igitur, sodes.
  Say (it) then   if you want

— Hoc totum constitit mihi sex quadrantibus.
  This   all   has stood to me six   farthings
                  (cost)

— Profecto fortuna tibi pulchre favit.
  Really   fortune you   pretty has favoured

— Quam mihi fortunam narras?
  Which to me   fortune   do you talk about

— Hic   mos   est loquendi.
  This a custom is   of speaking
        (way)

— "Mos" (ut dicitur) "tyrannus est pessimus". Atque
  Custom (as is said)   tyrant   is   the worst   And

utinam   bonos   mores   tam   studiose   coleremus,
would be   the good   customs   so   assiduously   we cultivate
(as)

quam obstinate retinemus malos!
as   obstinately   we keep to   the bad (customs)

— Tunc melius   se   haberent omnia.
Then   better   themselves would have all things
                would be in a state

— Nos igitur fortunam istam   Ethnicis   et
we   So   fortune   that   to the pagans   and

impiis   relinquamus. "Fortuna nihil est; solus
ungodly people   let us leave   Fortune   nothing   is   alone

est Deus, qui favet nobis,   solus   est adiutor et
it is God who favours us   (He) alone is   helper and

protector noster."
protector   our

— Sed audio signum   dari,   desinamus.
But   I hear   the sign to be given   let us cease

Part X

XLII.   HORARIUM   PUERI SCHOLARIS, I
42   The daily schedule of a boy   school-   1

— Hodie   mane   quota hora expergefactus
Today   in the early morning   at what   hour   been awoken

es?
you are
(have)

— Ante lucem; quota hora nescio.
Before (day)light at what   hour I do not know

— Quis te expergefecit?
Who   you   awoke

—   Venit   excitator   hebdomadarius   cum
Has come   the wake-up person   for the week   with

laterna   sua,   pulsavit   acriter   ostium
lantern   his   he has knocked   forcefully   (on) the door

cubiculi;   quidam   aperuit;   excitator
of the sleeping quarters somebody has opend the wake-up person

accendit   nostram   lucernam;   clara   voce
has kindled   our   oil-lamp   with a loud   voce

inclamavit. Experrecti sunt omnes.
he has cried out Woken up   are   all
                       (have)

— Narra mihi ordine quid   egeris   ex   illo
   Tell   me   in order what you have done from that

tempore usque ad finitum ientaculum. Vos pueri,
time   until   to the finished breakfast   You   boys
          until   breakfast had finished

auribus   atque   animis   diligenter   attendite,
with your ears and   minds   diligently   pay attention
{auris5pl}

ut   discatis   hunc   vestrum condiscipulum
in order that you learn   this   your   fellow pupil

imitari.
to imitate

— Experrectus sum,   surrexi e   lecto,   indui
   Woken up   I am I have risen from the bed I have put on
           (have)

115

tunicam cum thorace, sedi in scabello,
my garment with the doublet I have sat down on (my) footstool

accepi femoralia et tibialia, utraque
I have taken (my) breeches and (my) stockings both

indui, calceos calceavi, femoralia ligulis
I have put on (my) shoes I have drawn on the breeches with straps

astrinxi thoraci, tibialia periscelide
I have tied to my doublet the stockings with a leg-band

ligavi super crura, cingulo me praecinxi,
I have bound over my lower legs with a belt myself have girded
{crus1pl}

caput diligenter pexui, aptavi capiti
(my) head diligently I have combed I have put on (my) head

pileolum, togam indui; deinde egressus
(my) cap (my) toga I have put on thereupon having gone out of

cubiculo descendi infra,
the dormitory I went down below
I have descended to the ground floor

urinam in area reddidi ad parietem,
urine on the premises I have given back against the wall
I urinated in the yard

accepi aquam frigidam e situla, manus et
I have taken water cold from a jar the hands and

faciem lavi, os et dentes collui,
the face I have washed the mouth and the teeth I have rinsed

detersi mantili manus et faciem.
I wiped off with a towel hands and face

— Interea signum ad precationem datur minore
Meanwhile the signal for the prayer is given by the little

tintinnabulo. In aulam privatam convenitur,
bell To the hall private people are assembled

precamur una. Accipimus ordine ientaculum a
we pray together We receive in order breakfast from

famulo culinario, ientamus in triclinio
the manservant kitchen- we take breakfast in the triclinium
the cook

sedentes quieti, sine murmure et strepitu.
sitting quietly without buzz and noise

Quos audivi inepte garrientes, aut verba
(Those) who I have heard senseless talking or words

loquentes   otiosa,   aut   etiam   lascivientes   vidi,
speaking   idle   or   even   wantonly   I have seen

amice   admonui.   Qui   non   paruerunt
friendly   I have warned   (Those) who   not   have heeded

admonitioni,   detuli   ad   observatorem,   ut
the warning   I have denounced   to   the monitor   that

eos   notaret.
them   he would record

—   Nemone   vobis   praeerat   dum
        Nobody   to you   was in charge   while

ientaretis?
you people took breakfast

—   Imo   hypodidascalus.
        To the contrary   the undermaster

— Quid   agebat   interea?
What   did he do   in the meantime

— Ille   per   mediam   aulam   ambulabat   tenens
   He   through   the middle   hall   walked around   keeping
              through the hall

librum in manibus, et identidem monens
a book in (his) hands and now and then instructing

observatorem, ut notaret inepte garrientes.
the monitor that he should record senseless those talking

— Nullumne igitur verbum tunc licet emittere?
No at all so word then it is allowed to send out
(utter)

— Imo licet; verum ii demum
To the contrary it is allowed but they only

notari solent, qui diu et multis
to be taken down use who for a long time and with many

verbis inepte et sine ullo fructu confabulantur.
words senseless and without any profit talk together

Caeterum licet omnibus iucundos inter
Apart from that it is allowed to all pleasant among

se tractare sermones de bonis et
themselves to conduct conversations about good and

honestis rebus, dum tamen id modeste
honest matters while however that with moderation
(provided that)

fiat,   citra   clamorem   et   contentionem.
be done   at this side   noise   and   strife
       (without)

—   Hactenus   satisfecisti   mihi.   Caetera
     This far   you have satisfied   me   the other things

narrabis   a   prandio,   nisi   aliquod   negotium
you will tell   from   dinner   unless   some   business
       (after)

intervenerit.   Eamus   nunc   in   aulam   ad   prandium,
has come between   Let us go   now   into   the hall   for   dinner

ne   magistro   in   mora   simus.
that not   to the Master   in   delay   we are
           we hold up

—   Audivi   modo   signum   dari.
    I have heard   just   the signal   to be given

—   Opportune   datum.
    in the right moment   given

XLIII.   HORARIUM   PUERI   SCHOLARIS, II
   43   The daily schedule   of a boy   school-

—   Ubi   finivisti   narrationem   ante   prandium?
   Where   have you finished   (your) tale   before   dinner

— Cum vellem finem imponere de ientaculo, tu
When *I would* *an end* *to put* *about* *the breakfast* *you*

me interpellasti, praeceptor.
me *interrupted* *teacher*

— Perge igitur narrare ordine reliqua.
Go ahead *so* *to tell* *in order* *the rest*

— Dum ientandi finem facimus, datur
While *of (to) breakfasting* *an end* *we make* *is given*

publicum signum posterius. Sumit quisque libros;
the public (general) *signal* *later (second)* *takes* *everybody* *(his) books*

imus in aulam communem; recitantur
we go *into* *the hall* *common* *are read aloud*

de more catalogi singularum classium;
from custom / according to custom *the lists of names* *of the single* *classes {classis2pl}*

qui adsunt, ad nomen respondent; ego
those who *are present* *to* *(their) name* *answer* *I*

quoque respondeo; absentes notantur in catalogis
too *answer* *those absent* *are recorded* *in* *the lists*

121

ab ipsis nomenclatoribus. Finita catalogorum
by those who call out the names / Having ended / of the lists

recitatione, ludimagister pulpitum ascendit, ut
the reading out / the schoolmaster (head) / the pulpit / ascends / that (to)

precetur. Iubet nos attentos esse, tumque publice
he prays (pray) / he orders / us / attentive / to be / and then / publicly

precatur.
he prays

— **Ubi precatus est, Recipite, inquit, vos in**
Where (when) / prayed / is (has been) / Proceed / he says / you / to

suum quisque auditorium. Conveniunt omnes,
his own / each / auditory / They come together / all

ego item venio cum meis condiscipulis; sedeo in
I / same (too) / I come / with / my / fellow pupils / I sit down / in

loco meo. Praeceptor ingreditur; inquirit de
place / my / The teacher / comes in / he asks / about

absentibus; deinde sedet in cathedra sua, et
the absent / thereupon / he sits down / in (on) / seat / his / and

iubet — orders
pronuntiari — to be pronounced
auctoris — of the author
scriptum. — the writing

Pronuntiavimus — We pronounce it
terni — three at a time
clara — with a loud
voce, — voice
ut — as

solemus — we are used (to do)
quotidie. — daily
Tum — Then
iubet — he orders
ut — that
reddamus — we give

interpretationem. — an interpretation
Aliquot — Some
ex — out of
rudioribus — the fresher pupils
legunt, — read

singuli. — one at a time
Nos — We
alii — the others
reddimus — give it
terni, — three at a time
idque — and that

memoriter, — by heart
praeter — except
eum — him
qui — who
verba — the words
ipsa — themselves

auctoris — of the author
praeit — recites first
nobis — to us
ordine. — in order

— Tandem — At last
praeceptor — the teacher
exigit — requires
Gallicam — French (in Fr)
verborum — of the words

significationem. — the meaning
Respondent — They answer (Answer)
doctiores, — the more learned ones

quibus **nominatim** **id** **praecepit.** **Ego** **quoque**
to whom / by name / that / he has commanded / I / too

iussus **ab** **eo** **respondeo.** **Laudat** **illos** **qui** **bene**
ordered / by / him / give answer / He praises / those / who / well

responderint, **de** **quorum** **numero** **ego** **(quod** **sine**
have answered / from / whose / number / I / what / without

iactantia **dictum** **sit)** **unus** **eram.** **Postea** **iubet**
boasting / said / be {coni} / one / was / After that / he orders

singulas **orationis** **partes** **ordine** **tractari**
the single / of the text / parts / in order / to be treated

ad **rationem** **Grammaticam.** **Postremo** **palam**
(according) to / the rule / grammatical / Last of all / plainly

praescribit, **quid** **sit** **a** **prandio** **reddendum.**
he prescribes (tells) / what / is / from {coni} / dinner (after) / to be rendered

Audita **hora** **octava,** **precationem** **imperat;** **qua**
heard / hour / the eighth / a prayer / he commands / which

finita, **monet** **ut** **officium**
having been finished / he admonishes (us) / that / (our) duty

sedulo	faciamus.	Tandem	nos	missos	facit.
assiduously	we do	Finally	us	sent	makes
			he dismisses us		

Eo	spectante,	eximus	ordine	et	sine
With him	looking on	we go out	in order	and	without

strepitu,	laetique	discedimus.
noise	and glad	we leave

– Satisne	tibi	feci,	praeceptor?
Enough	for you	I have done	teacher
Have I satisfied you?			

– Imo	cumulatissime.
Yes, even	most abundantly

– Placetne	tibi	ut	sub	coenae	tempus	idem
Does it please	to you	that	under (during)	supper	time	the same

faciam	de	reliquis	huius	diei	actionibus?
I would do	about	the remaining	of this	day	doings

– Nihil	opus	erit.	Nam	de	iis	quae
Nothing	need	there is	For	about	those things	which
It is not at all needed						

horis	pomeridianis	aguntur,	alias	te
in the hours	afternoon	are done	another time	you

audivi   satis.
I have heard   enough

— Nunquid   vis   praeterea?
   anything   do you want   besides

— Estne tempus eundi in aulam communem ad
   Is it   time   to go   into   the hall   common   to

Psalmorum cantionem?
of the Psalms   the singing

— Tempus est. Ito igitur.
   Time   it is   Go   therefore

XLIV.   DANIEL   INSTRUCTIONEM
44   Daniel   instruction

EXTRA-ORDINARIAM RECIPIT
   extraordinary   receives

— Attende, Daniel, ut   discas   Latina   bene
   Pay attention   Daniel   that   you may learn   Latin (words)   well
   {imp}

Anglice vertere.
English   to turn into
{adv}

— Attendo   praeceptor.
I pay attention   teacher

— At diligenter.
But   diligently

— Imo diligentissime, et ex   animo.
Even   most diligent   and from   heart
                                    sincerely

— Bene facis.
Well   you do

— Propone igitur mihi   Latina,   ut   nobis
Put before   so   to me   the Latin (words)   as   to us
(Present)

interdum   soles.
now and than you use (to do)

— Quid   opus   est?
What   need(ed)   is

— "What is needed"?

— Gallinae
For a hen

— "To a hen".

— Ut
That

— "That".

— Illa
That
{f}

— "She".

— Sit
It be
{coni}

— "May be".

— Bona
Good
{f or n pl})

— "Good".

— Recte   fecisti.   Nunc ad singulas partes huius
Rightly you have done Now   to the single parts   of

orationis responde nominatim.
the   answer   namewise
                     (giving the name)

— Respondebo quoad   potero,   dummodo mihi
I will answer as far as I will be able provided that to me

praeieris.
you recite (them) first

— Quid
What

— Est nomen.
It is   a noun

— Opus
needed

— Nomen.
A noun

— Est
Is

— Verbum.
  A verb

— Gallina
  Chicken

— Nomen.
  A noun

— Ut
  That

— Coniunctio, in hoc loco.
  A conjunction in this place

— Illa
  That one
  {f}

— Pronomen.
  A pronoun

— Sit
  May be

— Verbum.
  A verb

— Bona
Good
{f}

— Nomen.
A noun

— Age, dicamus iterum, ut singula paulo
Come on let us say (it) again that the single (words) a bit

plenius intelligas.
more fully you understand

— Quid nunc respondebo?
What now will I answer

— Indica breviter singularium partium
Indicate in short single of the parts
{2pl}

declinatum, ut vos docere soleo.
the inflected form as you to teach I use

— Praeito igitur ut coepisti.
Recite first then as you have begun

— Quid
What

— "Quid, cuius", nomen substantivum anomalum.
What of what a noun substantive irregular

— Opus
Need

— "Hoc opus operis", ut "hoc onus oneris".
This need of the need like This load of the load

— Falleris, Daniel.
You are mistaken Daniel

— Quid ita.
Why so

— Quia "opus" hic est adiectivum.
Because need here is an adjective

— Eho, adiectivum! Quomodo declinatur?
Of an adjective How is it declined

— Est indeclinabile.
It is indeclinable

— Me miserum! Nunquam istud audieram.
me poor Never that I had heard

— Addendum fuit, "quod sciam", vel "quod
   to be added   was   that   In know   or   what
                {pf}   (as far as)   {coni}

meminerim".
I remember

— Quamobrem?
  For what reason

— Quia fortasse audieras, sed memineras
  Because maybe you had heard but you remembered

male.
badly

— Fieri potest; sed perge (quaeso) me docere.
  Happen it can but go on (I ask) me to teach
    Maybe

Quid Anglice significat istud nomen?
What (in) English does mean that noun

— Non solet Anglice verti, nisi iunctum cum
  Not it uses into English to be turned if not joined with
    (usually)

verbo "Sum, es".
the verb I am you are

— Da exemplum.
Give an example

— Quotidie in ore habes exempla.
Daily in the mouth you have examples

— Nunc mihi non occurrunt.
Now to me not they occur

— Nonne soles dicere, et audire ex
Not you use to say and to hear (it) from

condiscipulis, "Opus est mihi charta, atramento,
(your) fellow pupils Need there is to me paper ink
I have need of {charta5}

pecunia", et similia?
money and the like

— Saepe dico, fateor, et saepe audio; sed parum
Often I say (it) I confess and often I hear but too little

adverto.
I give attention

— Nunc igitur adverte, et manda memoriae,
Now then pay attention and send (it) to memory
{imp} learn by heart

"Opus est   mihi pecunia ad libros emendos, "I
Need there is to me   money   for books to be bought
     I need   {pecunia5}

have need of money to buy books"; vel sic, "I
                                      or   thus

need money".

— Da   item   aliud exemplum, quaeso.
   Give in the same way another   example   I ask

— "Opus   est   tibi virgis, ut tua   expellatur
   Need   there is to you of sticks that your may be driven out

pigritia", "Thou hast need of rods, that thy laziness
 laziness

may be driven out".

— Fateor equidem, praeceptor, sed Deus (ut spero)
  I confess   for sure   teacher   but   God (as I hope)

mei miserebitur.
of me will have mercy

— Omnium miseretur Deus qui pie illum
Of all has mercy God who piously Him

invocant. Sed de nomine "Opus" iam satis
invoke But about the noun Need already enough

multa, quod ad vos attinet: ad caetera
many as far as to you concerns to the other things

redeo: "Est".
I go back Is

— "Sum, es, esse", verbum anomalum.
I am you are to be a verb irregular

— Gallina.
Chicken

— "Gallina, gallinae", ut "mensa, mensae".
Chicken of the chicken as the table of the table

— Ut
As
(that)

— Non declinatur, quia est coniunctio. Anglice,
Not it is declined because it is a conjunction. (In) English

"That, to the end that, for that".

— Illa
　That one
　{f}

—　　"Ille"　　　　generis　　　masculini;　　　"illa",
　　　That one　　of the gender　　masculine　　　that one
　　　　{m}　　　　　　　　　　　　　　　　　　　{f}

　foeminini,　　　　　"illud",　　neutrius.
of the feminine (gender)　That (thing)　of the neuter (gender)

— Declina　in　foeminino.
　Decline (it)　in　(the) feminine (gender)

—　"Illa,　　illius,　　　illi,"　　" etc.
　That one　of that one　to that one　　etc

— Sit
　Be it
　(enough)

— Iam　dictum　est.
　Already　been said　it is
　　　　　　　(has)

— Bona
　Good
　{f}

— "Bonus",   generis   masculini; "bona",   feminini;
   Good   of the gender   masculine   good   of the feminine

"bonum",   neutrius,   nomen adiectivum.
 good   of the neuter (gender)   noun   adjective

—   Confer ad exemplum.
   Compare (it) to   the example

— "Iustus,   iusta,   iustum; bonus, bona, bonum".
 Righteous righteous righteous good   good   good
   {m}   {f}   {n}   {m}   {f}   (n)

—   Nunc   mutuo   vos interrogate,   ut   plenius
   Now   mutually you   ask   that more fully
     (each other)   (test)

omnia   tractetis.
everything you may treat

www.ingramcontent.com/pod-product-compliance
Lightning Source LLC
LaVergne TN
LVHW011333080426
835513LV00006B/316